The ELEMENTS
of PRAYER

The ELEMENTS of PRAYER

learning to pray
in real life

JOE B. JEWELL

New World Library
Novato, California

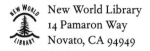 New World Library
14 Pamaron Way
Novato, CA 94949

Text design and typesetting by Tona Pearce Myers

Library of Congress Cataloging-in-Publication Data
Jewell, Joe B.
The elements of prayer : learning to pray in real life / Joe B. Jewell.
    p.   cm.
 ISBN-13: 978-1-57731-547-6 (hardcover : alk. paper)
1. Prayer. I. Title.
BL560.J49 2006
248.3'2—dc22   2006014343

First printing, October 2006
ISBN-10: 1-57731-547-2
ISBN-13: 978-1-57731-547-6

Printed in Canada on acid-free, partially recycled paper

g A proud member of the Green Press Initiative

Distributed by Publishers Group West

10 9 8 7 6 5 4 3 2 1

This book is dedicated to my parents, brother, and sister
for showing me the path,
and to my wife and children
for keeping me on it.

CONTENTS

PREFACE

I have been a parish minister for twenty-five years, and during that time the most common problem among my parishioners, the cause of their greatest consternation, has been prayer, or more accurately, praying. Actual questions about theology, liturgy, church positions, and scriptural meanings have arisen, but the question of how to pray appears the most. Everybody believes in it, thinks it works, and feels it's necessary to their life of faith and even life in general. But a lot of people do not think they really know how to do it.

I have been expected to pray a lot. I have frequently done it in the course of my work, be it in the expected moments during worship, the closing of a visit in the hospital, the grace for a church supper, or, my favorite, that impromptu moment when at the end of a meeting someone says, "let's close with prayer," and every head in the room turns to me. Whether practiced in private or before a group, prayer is one of the most expected and least explained events in religious life. During worship ample opportunities arise for public prayer, which the pastor usually leads: invocations, intercessions, celebrations, confessions, and pastoral prayers. Lay people often shy away from leading public prayer and seem bashful about discussing their private prayer. That's probably okay; we don't need to know how everyone else prays. However most people, whether new to or familiar with faith, are often stymied by the very idea of prayer.

Most people are scared of getting up in front of others. This fear is compounded when they are asked to pray in front of others. I once asked a parishioner to pray at the beginning of an important meeting. She initially declined, explaining she couldn't pray in front of that many people. I had heard her pray at a small women's group and knew she could do it. I laughed and said, "You think that many people will be there?

We better move to the sanctuary so we'll have more room." She got my meaning and agreed to open the meeting and did a beautiful job. More fundamentally, people are scared about praying in private because they are speaking to God. To me, if you can overcome the fear of speaking to God, praying in public should not be such a great hassle.

Prayer is fundamentally important to the life of faith. As ordinary as it may be for me, a professional pray-er, I must never forget that. Further, I must realize that it is precisely its fundamental importance that makes prayer so troubling for so many. In his wonderful essay "Teach Us to Care, and Not to Care," Eugene Peterson writes that teaching people to pray is a fundamental part of the life of faith, that "teaching people to pray is teaching them to treat all the occasions of their lives as altars on which they receive his gifts." It is in this spirit that I offer what follows.

There are many wonderful books about prayer, but not on prayer at its most fundamental. Whether you are new to or familiar with faith, whether you are trying to learn for yourself or help someone else learn, the best place to start is with the basics. This is my aim and hope in the following pages: to present a basic primer on how to pray — a starter and reminder to help us all.

INTRODUCTION

Ideas do not come from nowhere; even less do they spring full-blown into existence like Aphrodite from the head of Zeus. This little book has a history starting almost forty years ago when I first encountered *The Elements of Style* by William Strunk Jr. and E. B. White in my high school English classes. That elegant little manual of style has been a constant companion ever since — a concise, erudite guide to writing with clarity. A second influence was the warm reception I received when I paraphrased William Faulkner's Nobel Prize acceptance speech in a sermon a few years later. Over the years I have paraphrased other works in my sermons, such as changing John Wesley's Instructions for Singing into Instructions for Living. Time and interest brought me eventually to this idea of using Strunk and White's book as a model for a primer on learning to pray. The more I thought on it, the more it made sense. After all, prayer is expression, just as writing is, so what works for writing should work for praying.

We are all taught to write in school, but each of us takes to it differently and very few actually master the art. My brother once worked as the sports editor of a small town newspaper and one of the delivery workers approached him about doing some writing for the sports page. People had complimented this fellow on his writing ability and my brother, thinking another reporter couldn't hurt, told him to submit a trial article. The article my brother received simply did not measure up to publishable standards, but it was submitted on notebook paper in wonderfully clear and well-formed script. To his credit, my brother gently encouraged the man to pursue his current line of work while developing his writing skills.

As this story reminds us, we must constantly work on our ability to express ourselves. We must constantly refresh our skills in order to maintain and improve our abilities. Any baseball fan will tell you there is a world of difference between spring training and the playoffs. That is partly because spring training centers on fundamentals, sharpening the skills necessary for those important games in September. Writing or expressing one's ideas well needs constant work and a call to strong standards. Luckily, the more you practice writing and self-expression, the better you get.

What, you're asking yourself, does this have to do with prayer? Won't God know what I mean even if my words are awkward or unclear? Sometimes, but usually only in special cases: great grief, deep despair, joy beyond measure. Prayer, after all, is communication — intense, personal, intimate conversation with God. As such, it should be as clear and authentic as possible, because you are revealing your depths to God and to yourself.

Prayer begins with the assumption that we are praying to God. Whatever name you use, regardless of your particular faith, when you pray, you are praying to God. This is what stymies a lot of people. They are intimidated by the very idea of speaking to God. They think they somehow don't measure up; they feel unworthy of an audience with God. On numerous occasions I've had people come to me with a problem and say they won't be attending church until they get it worked out, that their situation makes them feel undeserving. I have learned to gently urge them to attend for just that reason. If everyone who felt unworthy stayed home, I tell them, no one would be there on Sunday morning, me included.

The same thinking is often applied to prayer and is the result of equating faith and morality. As Parker Palmer says in *Let Your Life Speak*, God is "the source of reality rather than morality, the source of what is, rather than what ought to be." Faith tells us that God accepts us, whatever our condition. To confront that condition, whatever it may be, we have to present it to God. Our faith is always relational; it lives only in relationship — and prayer is the fundamental conduit of that relationship.

So the first assumption of prayer is that you are praying to some "other," to God in whatever guise he or she appears to you. That is why it scares us so. If you are new to prayer, you'll likely be unsure how to start or what to say. It is similar to meeting someone to whom you are attracted. You are not quite sure what to say, how to make an approach. You don't know how he or she will respond or maybe judge you.

The second assumption of prayer is that God wants to hear what you have to say. My guess is that you wouldn't be reading this book if you hadn't already made this assumption. The assumptions that you are praying to God and God wants to hear your prayer are the twin pillars of faith; accepting them opens the door to the blessing and power of prayer.

What follows is a guide to help you express yourself clearly and fully in prayer. There are five chapters, based on the chapters in Strunk and White's *The Elements of Style*. The first chapter, "The Rules of Usage," addresses the fundamental question of what do we pray for? The second chapter, "The Principles of Composition," shapes the context for prayer and helps make it meaningful. The next two chapters are more cautionary: chapter three details some matters of form, what works and what sometimes doesn't, and the fourth chapter addresses some words and expressions that are easily misused and why that matters. Finally, chapter five, "An Approach to Prayer," is designed, like its model, to give anyone a compass for finding his or her own way. Along the way, examples of classic and contemporary prayers will illustrate each point.

I wrote many of the examples, not to show how good I am at it but to show you that anyone can do it. They are intended as positive guidelines. They are not intended to dictate how you should pray, though using them can't hurt. After all, Jesus offered the Lord's Prayer as an example, not as the only way to pray. (Yes, it's included here.) Maybe these prayers, especially the classics, will speak to you. Reading, even memorizing, them is helpful, but like any piece of honest self-expression their real value lies in enhancing the quality of your own communication. That is the aim of this book.

Like *The Elements of Style*, this book is not intended to be exhaustive but fundamental. It strives to outline rather than fill in so that the reader can find his or her own way of praying. The rules are directives, not strictures. The intention is to make plain and accessible what seems to many an arcane art. My hope is that the reader will become a pray-er and find himself or herself engaged in this essential element of life.

The ELEMENTS
of PRAYER

[1]

The RULES of USAGE

Almost instinctively, the first question we ask is "What do I pray for?" There are two kinds of praying: for purpose and for object. The first is concerned with the reason for praying while the second involves what the prayer asks for. The first recognizes that all prayers have an intention and the second that all prayers are petitions. The rules of this section seek to answer both sides of the question "What do I pray for?" in such a way that praying stays centered on its primary function: relating to the Great Other.

1. Pray for yourself.

This is not being selfish; this is where you start. Fundamentally, prayer is about your relationship with God. You are the one communicating, and central to that communication is putting yourself in relationship with God. The real you must be present — no one else, no others, no false selves. This is your expression and yours alone. Too many people use false humility to avoid praying. "I'm too bad to pray" or "I don't know what to pray about." Others simply try to fool God by pretending to be other than who they really are. This is the one communication where it is utterly safe to be who you really are. God expects your true self to show up.

One of the best examples of being your true self in prayer comes in the closing moments of the movie *Cool Hand Luke* when, trapped in a church, the serial escapee Luke turns to God and prays to "the Old Man." His prayer is completely in character: direct, honest, and totally congruent with who he is. He isn't afraid that God will reject that self. (He is also not really sure whether it is worth praying.) When I first saw this scene in a theater many years ago, I was startled by its directness. Here were no formal addresses, no stultifying language, no pieties — just direct, real speech. Nothing comes between Luke and "the Old Man." It is just the two of them, two selves interacting. It changed my long-standing attitude that prayer was formal and impersonal and made it more realizable for me.

Similarly, a young mother drew me aside one Sunday after church to discuss a problem. We stood in my office, with me itching to get out of my robes and stole and get a cup of coffee. "This prayer thing doesn't seem to be working for me," she told me. I asked her to explain. She listed the things she prayed for and explained how she saw no improvements in any of them. I was about to give her a standard answer involving the inscrutability of God's intentions when she added, "I'm not sure God cares about me." That stopped me cold. I asked her if she had prayed about that uncertainty. She replied she had not, that it seemed selfish, unworthy. I realized that prayer was external to her, a form to be filled out and sent in, her spiritual income tax. I told her that what she needed to pray about was how she kept God at arm's length. I explained that prayer was about relating to God and making that relationship more central to her prayer would help it become more meaningful to her. We agreed to meet again and after a few follow-up talks she began to feel more comfortable with prayer.

The self who prays is both the intention and the object of the prayer. God accepts the real you and will respond to who you are, so the real you has to show up. It is simply the way it works.

> O God, my needs seem so small, so insignificant when compared to yours. Hear my prayer and open your heart as I open mine. I bring who I am, who I hope to be. Dwell in me that I might dwell in the world as you intend me to be. Let your will for me become my desire. Let me be your prayer to the world.
>
> Amen.

2. *Pray for your concerns.*

Whatever most occupies your consciousness is your true concern. The events, worries, problems, joys, and excitements of your life are the first things you should mention in prayer. They are easiest to pray about because they sit at the forefront of your awareness. You don't have to spend a lot of time thinking up stuff to pray about; you simply start with "this bothers me" or "this excites me."

Identifying what most concerns you helps you face what most concerns you. This is the old tactic of "naming the demon." When you identify your problems you take a major step toward handling them. Praying won't necessarily resolve your vexing concerns, but it will help you identify them and keep them in perspective. Once you start the process you will find yourself sorting out what does and doesn't really concern you. In other words, your worries will be given priority and you'll find them more manageable. The first requirement is being honest with yourself. That commitment points you in the right direction from the outset.

I was once attended a clergy luncheon about race relations. The convening clergyman, who happened to be white, closed the meeting with a prayer. We had discussed both national and local race issues during the day and the group, which was made up of many different races, had a fruitful and helpful gathering. However, as the minister prayed I felt a poke in my side from the friend and colleague who sat beside me. He rolled his eyes and shook his head. He knew I was thinking the same thing he was. Afterward, in the safety of the parking lot, we talked about our disrespectful reaction. The prayer was the way to close the meeting, but its content and delivery belied its sincerity. His tone was condescending, he used pat phrases that didn't ring authentic, and the whole effort felt out of key. In the words of my friend, he was faking it; there was no real concern about race in his words. To me with my Southern heritage he sounded like "Massa extolling the good darkies." That is not the kind of prayer you present to God when you really care. Think about it: when something really concerns you it is clear in your language and tone. God deserves no less.

> Keep me focused, O God, upon my troubled heart. Help me hear the cries of concern that echo there and help me strive after the path of resolution that you would have me follow. May your Love be my watchword, and my life be a help to those in need through your strength.
>
> Amen.

3. Pray for what counts.

Once you have identified your concerns, you then have to determine what you can and can't do about them. You have to understand the connection between what you are feeling and how to turn that feeling into appropriate action. Good prayer always helps. Once you identify your true concerns, you can generally fig-ure out how to act. This is what counts. You can pray all you want about world peace for example. You can tell God that you want the world to be at peace until you are blue in the face and God probably is too. This may make you feel better, but it is a shallow feeling, one without staying power.

The next question is crucial: "What can I do to

promote world peace?" Then you began to see your way forward. Maybe you'll study geopolitical realities in order to promote what you believe to be the best course of action, or you may create some work of art to inspire others toward world peace, or you may resolve personally to act nonviolently with all you encounter. Whatever you choose, and it is entirely your choice, it will open up possibilities and opportunities for acting for world peace. Then your good feeling will have results and have depth and your life will be enriched.

This is virtually what I told a man in one parish when he presented me with this very problem. I had included the problem of world peace in a sermon as an illustration of how faith works in the world and he pressed the issue of how action proceeds from faith. He understood that world peace wouldn't bend to his will, but he didn't understand why it wouldn't. "Maybe you should start with your understanding," I told him, "and work out how your understanding can lead to responsible action. Then you can find what you can do to promote peace." And he did.

Praying for what counts helps to identify your place in the world, your role in life. It determines your relationship to your concerns: whether you let them run your life or whether you understand and fruitfully handle them. Praying for what counts doesn't put you in charge, it merely helps you see your relationship to other influences in the world, and what it is possible to change. Sometimes what counts is simply the praying itself.

> Lord, make me an instrument of your peace! Where there is hatred, let me sow love; where there is injury, pardon; where there is doubt, faith; where there is despair, hope; where there is darkness, light; and where there is sadness, joy.
>
> O Divine Master, grant that I may seek to be consoled as to console; to be understood as to understand; to be loved as to love; for it is in giving that we receive; it is in pardoning that we are pardoned; and it is in dying that we are born to Eternal Life.
>
> — St. Francis of Assisi

4. *Pray for reality.*

How do you pray for reality? Reality is what it is and some people question whether prayer can affect reality. Others of course think prayer is the only reality. The truth, as usual, lies somewhere in between. The issue at stake in prayer is our relationship to reality. What we pray for is to understand reality for what it is and not what we think it is. We should not use prayer to try to confirm what we think is real. Instead, prayer should humbly seek to understand the way things are.

We all make certain assumptions about reality. Prayer should question those assumptions. Prayer may confirm their trustworthiness or reveal their flaws. Either way you are better off. You can either move confidently forward or search for new and more accurate assumptions.

Once while sitting around with a group of young people in one of my churches, one of the young men asked me, "What is real?" Being a bit of a smart-ass, especially in an informal setting, I gave him a glib answer like "cheese whiz." He laughed, and we played with the idea, but something in his manner told me the question wasn't meant facetiously. A little later when the others had left, I probed a little deeper. He wanted to know how one could distinguish what was real from what just appeared to be real or others believed to be real. That led to a long, deep, involved conversation about the nature of reality and the role of faith in finding one's place in that reality.

Knowing his family story and some worries his stepmother had shared with me, I understood there were underlying issues to his question. I wanted to help him find a place to stand in the midst of life, during a time when everything seems in flux and turmoil. I knew we had found it when he latched onto the idea that asking ourselves serious questions is like asking God serious questions. He realized it was okay to question God, and with that he realized that reality was bigger than he could fathom. It helped that he was a very good science student, and we could talk about Heisenberg's uncertainty principle, the idea that the observation of a phenomenon affects the phenomenon itself. He could understand that reality can be very slippery. I told him that real prayer is asking to know God without preconceived notions about what God might be. This is praying for reality.

This is a hard rule to follow because we expend a lot of our mental and spiritual energy establishing, defending, and promoting our personal notions of reality. Using patience and time and discipline to question our assumptions will help us ground ourselves more firmly in God's reality.

Teach us, O Holy One, your way again. From great to small your heart roams, seeking the fulfillment of all. But we stumble, get lost, and fail to pay attention; we let our doubts overwhelm us.

Remind us that the road to your peace is a humble one, that our understanding relies on you. It is your light upon our dark path we seek.

Amen.

5. *Pray for direction.*

People often say, "I prayed and I still don't know what to do" or "I prayed but didn't get an answer." This is when two old adages about prayer come to bear: (1) Be careful what you pray for because you might get it and (2) God always answers prayer, it just might not be the answer you wanted. The hidden assumption these adages reveal is that prayer is about answers. It's important to remember that prayer is simply about prayer. You pray to the Great Other in order to maintain and build your relationship. That relationship shapes who you are and that identity moves you to act. The concerns of your life then receive the attention they need and are resolved.

Prayer is not some magic bullet you can go to for answers, solutions, or reassurances that you are right. It is not asking God to solve your problems or answer your questions or magically heal you like some kind of mystical ombudsman. I was violently disabused of such notions one Sunday morning in the fourth grade. I was sitting in Sunday school when I felt my stomach go awry. I rushed into the bathroom and closed myself in a stall. When my stomach continued to roil, I prayed I wouldn't be sick. I prayed with all my might and promised God I'd do anything: never be bad again, dedicate my life to His work. I then proceeded to lose the entire contents of my stomach and then some.

I figured that if prayer didn't work in Sunday school, it probably didn't work anywhere. The fact that I've spent over thirty years studying and pursuing God's meaning is the ironic twist on this story. That prayer didn't help my stomach virus, but it may well have been a key point in turning my life toward the pursuit of faith and religious meaning.

Direction comes when we consciously seek it. Prayer seeks guidance for how we are to proceed, the best way to live out what our faith tells us is important. Asking for resolutions or answers or healing may be a part of that seeking, as long as our search for answers rests on the best intentions we can have for ourselves and others. Just lining up our intentions with God's intentions works to our advantage, but it doesn't necessarily mean our original intentions will be fulfilled. (Again, God does answer prayer, just not always with the answer we expect.) As we line ourselves up in that hope of living out God's intentions, we establish the direction of our lives. The answers, the solutions, the healings, and the celebrations of our lives will become apparent as we move along that path.

I'm tired of the runaround, God. Too much that means too little clogs my way. I feel lost, even abandoned, in the midst of my life. Help move me toward something again. Give me a clear eye to help spot the way I must go and help me find the strength I need to take those steps. May your will for me become my heart and may your love become mine, so that I am eternally seeking my place in your kingdom.

Amen.

6. *Pray for what you seek.*

This is not the same thing as what you want. Wants are bound to the things of this world. You want a new car or house or the tools back that your neighbor borrowed. Wants naturally accrue to us through living and are determined by what we experience and learn and see beyond our grasp. However, wants will pass and be replaced by others. They are transitory by nature. That does not make them bad. We all have them and must learn to handle them and prevent them from ruling our lives.

Wants symbolize a deeper part of us, namely what we ourselves long to be, what we are to become. What we seek is the person we are meant to be, given all the factors that have converged on our being. Author Joseph Campbell's mythic motif of the hero's journey in his book *The Hero with a Thousand Faces* plots the course that seeking takes: the call beyond routines, the adventures along the way, the friends met and obstacles overcome, and the struggle to obtain the boon (what we seek) and bring it back to our regular world. The point is we all seek to be the person we are meant to be. How we achieve that is as varied as we are, but the quest is universal. What we seek in prayer should be an understanding of that boon. Our wants may symbolically represent that deeper seeking, but they should not overwhelm it. That is ultimately unsatisfying and frustrating.

One time a man came to my office wanting to talk about "things." As a pastor I've learned over the years to pick up on the nonverbal signs of trouble people give off and this guy was giving off a lot of them. I knew he was having problems in his marriage before he sat down. He told me he wanted to have an affair. I asked him why; he had a lovely wife of some twelve years. What was driving him toward an affair? He responded that his life seemed so routine, so normal, so common, so dull. There was no adventure or excitement anymore. The thought of an affair excited him. It was dangerous, it was fun, and so on. So why come see me? Why not seek out a willing partner? That gave him pause, and he launched into a long, winding explanation that ended with him basically admitting he felt guilty for thinking these things. I asked him if he came to me to get rid of the guilt or the idea. He didn't know.

He was suffering from a lack of imagination, and I

told him so. What he sought was to feel vibrant and exciting, and that translated into the idea of an affair. "Use your imagination," I said. "Have an affair with your wife." Luckily, things worked out for them. An extramarital affair seemed like it would satisfy his longing, but it would only have produced a transitory satisfaction and probably a world of hurt. By recognizing what he sought beneath his transitory desire, he actually improved his marriage.

I remember the tent revivals of my youth where the revivalist would sometimes pray for a new Cadillac. It was easy to make fun of praying for a luxury car, but when you recognize that it represents someone seeking what God wants of him or her, you realize more is going on than you might have first assumed. Use your prayer to seek what God intends you to be, to seek your true home, to seek what you most want to be. That will keep your desires in perspective.

> Thou hast made us for thyself, O Lord; and our heart is restless until it rests in thee.
>
> — St. Augustine

7. Pray for the present.

You don't live anywhere but the present. So you pray to be fully in, and focused on, the present. That is why in the best known of all Christian prayers, the one Jesus presented as a model for prayer, He uses the phrase "give us this day." It anchors our devotion to the present moment. The tense of the Lord's Prayer is present: who art, kingdom come, be done, give, forgive, lead, deliver. No promises presented for future gain, no past lapses mulled over. Prayer happens now, not then. You have to be present in this moment as fully as you can.

Understand that if your prayer is addressed to God, what you are doing, or at least attempting to do, is entering God's time. We call that time eternity. As author Frederick Buechner points out, eternity is not the opposite of time but its essence. To enter God's time is to accept that the Great Other is always available. In God's time, God is present. The Great Other is not hiding somewhere way off in the future, "down Eternity's road." God is available now.

At the annual regional gathering of my denomination, where we set policy, budgets, and such, I was once unexpectedly asked by the convener of a discussion group to offer an opening prayer. We were going to discuss a thorny issue with many strong and opposed positions. When called upon, I first asked for silent prayer, as much to give myself time to think as to settle everyone down and promote a peaceful atmosphere. Then, I simply asked God to be with us in our discussion so that at our conclusion we might reflect His will. Afterward, an older woman thanked me, saying the prayer reminded her that we can only expect to find God among us right now, and we shouldn't worry about whether He'll be with us down the line.

So, we pray now and focus on this moment. How we conduct ourselves in any given moment usually determines how we will live in the next. Prayer then is practice for living and, more important, practice for what it is like to live in God's present, in God's time. Practice makes doing easier. Practicing through prayer makes living in the Great Other's present more achievable. In fact, it is when living in God's time starts.

> Our Father, who art in heaven, hallowed be thy name. Thy kingdom come. Thy will be done on earth as it is in heaven. Give us this day our daily bread, and forgive us our trespasses as we forgive our trespassers. Lead us not into temptation, but deliver us from evil. For thine is the kingdom and the power and the glory, forever.
> Amen.
> — Traditional version based on Matthew 6

8. Pray for God's presence.

Prayer is a time when everything else stops. All you are doing is praying. (At least that is the idea.) All the activities, relationships, emotions, hope, joys, and concerns that compose your life can be included in prayer, but what you are doing is offering all of that to God, asking that God's presence come into the actions of your life through you. This equation can be turned around as well. You become the presence of the Great Other in the world through living and acting in a particular way, a way that embodies that presence. Christians call this incarnation, the spirit becoming flesh.

By all biblical accounts, being in God's presence is a pretty humbling experience, so if you don't feel humble when you are praying, then you are probably doing something wrong, like not being honest. One of my favorite examples of this is the story of Elijah on Mount Horeb. Elijah is fresh from a spectacular victory over the prophets of Baal and Queen Jezebel is seeking to kill him. So he hides out on Mount Horeb and calls on Yahweh to help him much like he did with Baal's boys. However, his manner is a problem; he puts himself at the center of the show. He gets an answer but not the one he was expecting. First comes enough wind to blow him down, then thunder to deafen him, and finally an earthquake to shake him up, but Yahweh's presence is not in them. Finally, in the silence after all the brouhaha, Yahweh's presence is there. Maybe the silence is the presence. Elijah gets the idea. God doesn't jump through hoops for anyone, and shows up as only Yahweh can when Yahweh chooses. This silence is more humble than earthquakes and thunder, but it gets the job done. The first requisite for entering that presence is humbly seeking it.

Being in that presence gives meaning and shape and form to our lives. In his essay "Teach Us to Care, and Not to Care," Eugene Peterson delineates how seeking and recognizing the presence of God in the midst of life transforms life. If you pray honestly and humbly, it starts a process where living and praying hopefully become indistinguishable. That is what it's like to be in God's presence.

> When I see, Lord, let it be with your heart.
> When I speak, let your words ring out.
> When I hear, let me know who speaks.
> When I judge, let your Love reign.
>   Amen.

9. Pray for vision.

Vision is often misrepresented these days. When we speak of it, we refer to the ability to see ahead, to project a course of action. Such clairvoyance is fine except that it is not born *sui generis*, of itself. It arises from our current context with all its limitations. To accurately see where you are headed, you must first determine where you are. Any good, or even mediocre, sailor will tell you that you plot your course by first determining your position on the chart. So, when I say we must pray for vision, I literally mean seeing what is around us.

I choose the preposition *around* very carefully. We need to see as accurately as possible, as honestly as possible, all that is around us, and we need to identify just as accurately and just as honestly our relationship to that reality. When we pray for vision we are praying to comprehend our self, what counts, what is real, what way lies ahead, what we seek, what is present — God's presence and our own. What we are trying to see when we pray for vision is our own part, role, and place in the totality of existence. We are praying to see that existence as a whole, to understand it as an endeavor that has meaning and is rooted in the Great Other's intentions for the world. We pray for vision that gives our own lives a sense of belonging in that existence.

Early in my pastoral career, a woman was struggling with the recent loss of her mother. She felt angry but didn't feel like she could express that anger to God in her prayers. From somewhere, I found the inspiration to tell her to take another look at God. A lot worse things than her anger had been sent His way. He was big enough to handle her anger. She needed the vision to see God as accepting of her and her anger, and loving her not one bit less.

As we move toward that kind of vision, we move toward that same acceptance of ourselves and our lives. We see ourselves in some sense as God sees us, and we come to accept ourselves hopefully as God accepts us, warts and all. This is acceptance, not acquiescence. Acquiescence means giving up some part of yourself, changing in order to be accepted (by God or anyone else), instead of knowing that who you are is accepted. Any change for the better starts from true acceptance. Acquiescence is accomplished only with some resentment, some feeling of loss. Acceptance brings a feeling of wholeness.

Note well, it is vision you seek, not visions; it is a path into the future, not dreams ungrounded by reality. The true role of the Old Testament prophets was not simply to predict the future, but to describe the present situation from Yahweh's perspective and point at the future it would, or could, produce.

Once you see or even begin to see what is around you in that honest and humble way, once you begin to see clearly, the way to go becomes more and more apparent. The way, as the Quakers say, will open before you.

> Help me, O God, to discern the whole of your creation in the moments of my life. Give me a judgment centered on your will for all and each. May my knowing, my loving, my valuing be determined not by my sight, but yours.
>
> Amen.

10. Pray for praying's sake.

Praying itself is worth the effort. It does not matter what deity or non-deity you believe in. If you pray, you are getting in touch with who you are and how you relate to the world; you are learning and practicing how to relate to the world. Prayer is practice for all life's meaningful communication. The more you do it, the better you get at it. If you take the time to communicate well, when you make the effort to be clear, you improve your ability to communicate all the time.

While attending graduate school, I worked in a theological library in downtown Boston. When I started there, the staff was four older ladies and me. I quickly became friends with all of them. I have always had a habit of talking to myself and one day I mentioned this to Velma, with whom I regularly worked. I knew I had found a substitute home when she replied in her gravelly voice, "You can't work here if you don't talk to yourself."

Prayer fills that bill. It is talking in a way that links you most fully to your life. Many times it feels like you are just talking to yourself, but prayer can lead to greater understanding or new insight or improved relations. You never know.

Prayer puts you into play with things other than you and thus in play with the Great Other. You begin to realize that this talking to yourself is reaching beyond yourself. Something within you makes contact with something beyond you. Prayer just helps you to pay enough attention to realize that the Great Other is responding. It takes time, but it is time well spent. The more you pray the better you get at it.

Prayer is the essence of communication because to be effective it demands that you be who you really are. By addressing your real self to another Self, the One in which you place ultimate faith, the One who is always Itself, the One who tells Moses His name is "I Am," you are finding your own place in the universe. From that point, everything else begins.

This is where we start, Lord. You and me.
Hear me and let me hear you. Let's talk.

About whatever is or might be. You and me.
Right now, this is all that matters.
Nothing else comes close.
Thanks for that, for you and me.
In the end that's what it comes down to.
All the rest is simply that. We speak, you and me.
   Amen.

[2]

The PRINCIPLES
of COMPOSITION

Once you know why you are praying and what you are praying for, you can start to think about how you pray. It is probably a mistake to assume the why and the what are settled forever. One thing life teaches us is that everything changes and praying can affect how we live and thereby change it. So the how, what, and why of praying are in a dynamic relationship; there is a cause and effect between them, just as there is between prayer and life.

This just means you have to be on your toes and

expect the effects of praying. The word I most associate with this attitude is *heuristic*, a great word I discovered reading the philosopher Michael Polanyi. It means to accept something as good for now until something better is found. Prayer is like that: you pray for all the right reasons and it moves you in a certain direction. Suddenly new possibilities present themselves and you involve yourself in them — and the cycle continues.

Using an effective technique can help prayer work. Composing a prayer is similar to preparing a favorite recipe: you know the ingredients and their amounts, you know the order in which to combine the ingredients, and you know the process of preparation. Composing prayers becomes easier and smoother the more you do it and, as in cooking, the quality and attention with which you prepare the ingredients of your prayer will be reflected in the final product. What follows are some basic rules to help compose prayers. Their aim is to make the how of prayer easier and more effective.

11. *Choose a suitable design and hold to it.*

This works for all kinds of prayers, public and private alike. Most liturgical prayers, prayers used in public worship, are identified as one of the following: confession, contrition, pardon, praise, intercession, invocation, benediction, illumination, or blessing. All are designs that fulfill certain functions. High liturgy churches (e.g., Roman Catholic, high church Anglican, some Lutheran) have designed these and others forms of prayers for particular uses. Prayer books and books of worship from various denominations are often organized, at least in part, around these designs, and it is instructive to consult one of these sources and read through the different prayers. You will find various expressions but common purpose running through the different denominational forms. This variety shows the myriad ways of praying about or for the same thing. During public prayer, these forms help keep everyone focused on the intent of the act.

Your private prayers do not have to follow these public forms, but it is important to remember that prayer is a focused activity. Whatever prompts you to pray, be it the need of a moment or a routine you follow, it is helpful to establish a design for your prayer. In the course of my parish career, I often find myself in a moment when private prayer is called for: at a hospital bedside, a visit on the anniversary of a death, or the celebration of a birth. I work to find appropriate prayers for each of these occasions. Even though I am trained for such moments, I take time to center my thoughts and design what I will say around the need of each occasion.

Similarly, the routine of daily prayer should have

its own design. As Strunk and White say, "foresee and determine the shape of what is to come and pursue that shape." There are ample aids for shaping daily prayer. Every denomination publishes daily prayer guides. Religious publishers of all kinds print many different forms as well, from prayer calendars to monthly magazines. Find the one that works for you and use it. The discipline of such daily devotion will build your confidence in prayer and strengthen your spiritual life. Yes, you will find that there are times when the best design is no design and you simply let things flow.

12. Make the paragraph the unit of composition.

In daily life, the human mind jumps from one thought to the next as it tries to keep up with our busy world. We tend to think in a rush of headlines or sound bites, not paragraphs. When praying you want to slow your mind and focus on the purpose of your prayer, allowing the initial headline of an idea to grow and expand into deeper, more detailed thoughts like a well-written essay. Focus is the key here. When you are praying you want the prayer alone to occupy your mind and soul. Remember, you are communicating with God! You want all your attention devoted to this effort. No thinking about the myriad number of things you need to do. Think and concentrate on this one thing. While you are praying take it one paragraph at a time. Present your thought, cover any relevant points, and move on to the next thought with the same focus.

Sometimes one paragraph is all you need. Once during my seminary days, I worked with an urban ministry program that oversaw a drug rehab program. One of the recovering addicts slid back into his drug habit and died of a heroin overdose. At the next meeting of the support group of which he was a part, we gathered in a circle to offer our prayers for him. One of the members, quoting a popular song, just said, "God, damn the pusher." It was enough.

Don't think of your prayer as one long, continuous monologue. Break the ideas down into digestible, understandable parts. This will help you to know what you are praying for. It will keep both your and God's attention focused on what is necessary in that moment.

13. Use the active voice.

My high school sophomore English teacher literally drummed the difference between active and passive voice into my head. When we covered the topic in class, erasers and chalk flew through the air. We soon learned that active voice was vigorous and direct; subjects produce action and don't receive it. So why would this be important for prayer?

It has to do with the habit of being active. The more you think and express yourself in an active way, the more likely you are to be active. The point of prayer, after all, is your life and how you live. Your prayers should help establish the habit of activity. Using the active voice provides great clarity about one's responsibility to take action. Prayer requires such clarity.

You are the subject of your prayer and when you are clear about this responsibility your prayer is more effective. You do not get to avoid that responsibility when you pray, which is probably one reason why prayer so scary to so many people. We know deep down that we can't fool God, that we are accountable to Him. That is why H. Richard Niebuhr, one the great twentieth-century theologians, insisted that the only proper stance before God was repentance.

The active voice engenders directness, is more definite, and more concise. Using the active voice in prayer helps us to live with action as well and avoid equivocation and denial. By practicing such directness in prayer we learn to be direct.

When praying publicly, the active voice provides a steady hand to steer with. "Brevity is a by-product of vigor," say Strunk and White, and the active voice supplies that vigor in speech and writing. It makes prayer shorter, more to the point, and more understandable.

14. Make statements affirmative.

Nobody really likes to be told what they are not, or for that matter, what is not. They like to hear what they are and what is. Couching statements in the negative communicates defensiveness and avoidance. Hesitant language avoids commitment.

"I am not sure that will work" and "I am sure that will not work" say the same thing, but the latter is positive and more forceful.

Not has its place. Used in denial — "Do not do that" — or antithesis — "That is not the case" — it is strong. Used to state something that can or should be, it is weak — "my computer should not have trouble with that."

We can make the case that God likes affirmative forms as well. Whenever someone in the Old Testament tried to hedge their bets with God they usually ended up in more trouble, Jonah being the most obvious example by ending up in the belly of a great fish. God's strongest and most direct statements in the Old Testament use positive language.

What about the Ten Commandments, you ask? Look again. The first five are positive. They are formative, the ones that tell what society and people should do to create a sustainable and just world. The second five are the "nots." They establish the prohibitions that help maintain the first five.

Positive language is the language of commitment and that is what God seeks from us. Throughout his ministry on earth, Jesus sought commitment from his disciples, his followers, and his listeners. He called constantly in his teaching for those who heard him to choose their own way.

When I was an undergraduate, I told one of my English professors that I had decided to enter the ministry. He looked at me askance and kind of snorted. All he heard from theological schools, he said, was doubt. They taught people how not to believe. His reaction took me aback and because I admired him I questioned my decision quite seriously. But he didn't change my mind, because he had not been talking about me. I knew what I was and what I wanted to pursue, so his negativity didn't convince me. I only wish I had known then Frederick Buechner's definition of doubt. "Doubt" writes Buechner "is the ants in the pants of faith." That's a fine example of turning a negative into a positive.

15. Use definite, concrete language.

First of all, it's good for you. Definite, concrete speech makes it hard to equivocate and avoid. It carries an enforced honesty. Prayer is the one place above all others where you want to be honest. You want to be honest about yourself, your concerns, and your hopes when you pray. Not because God would know if you were being dishonest, but because you don't want to lie to yourself. Prayer demands self-honesty. It is the only way it works.

Second, using definite, concrete language is good for God. It allows God to see and hear you straight up. There is no beating around the bush or avoiding the issues. If I may be bold, I believe that God appreciates that straightforward attitude. Jeremiah, the Old Testament prophet, didn't beat around the bush with God even though he often had some pretty harsh things to say. God could see him for what he was and gave him appropriate messages to deliver, which often were also pretty harsh. Your honesty with God opens the way for God to use you in the way that fits.

Third, definite, concrete language is good for others. When you are praying in public, such language avoids platitudes or vague sentiments that serve no purpose. It also engages the listener, makes it easier to pray along. Such definite expression helps others not only to grasp what you are saying and praying for, but also helps them pray on their own in the same way.

Strunk and White supply a wonderful example of concrete language by comparing a translation of the King James version of Ecclesiastes written by George

Orwell with the original biblical text to show the beauty of the Bible's concrete, direct language:

> Objective consideration of contemporary phenomena compels the conclusion that success or failure in competitive activities exhibits no tendency to be commensurate with innate capacity, but that a considerable element of the unpredictable must inevitably be taken into account.
>
> — George Orwell

> I returned, and saw under the sun, that the race is not to the swift, nor the battle to the strong, neither yet bread to the wise, nor yet riches to men of understanding, nor yet favor to men of skill; but time and chance happeneth to them all.
>
> — Ecclesiastes, King James Version

16. *Omit unnecessary words.*

This may be a universal rule. It is truly hard to think of a situation where it does not apply. As Strunk and White indicate, every word must tell. Unnecessary words just get in the way of clear, vigorous expression. Prayer is no different. The unnecessary just clouds the issue. Flowery and bombastic language, while impressive to the inattentive, disguises a lack of meaning for those seriously engaged in prayer. One beginning assumption is that God is engaged in prayer, and God is always attentive and not fooled by such language. The same goes for public prayer. Those listening will just be bored or irked by unnecessary language.

Public prayer should involve those who are present in the act of praying. Public prayer is not just someone standing in front of others praying about his or her concerns. Public prayer involves all those present. Vigorous speech engenders that involvement. So, the clutter must go.

Concise speech involves discipline and preparation. It takes time and dedication to create a public prayer that engages others. It also takes time and dedication to pray meaningfully on your own. This preparation is often the most significant part of the prayer. Experience over my pastoral career confirmed the wisdom a retired pastor shared with me at church camp when I was a teenager: "The preparing for prayer is most often the prayer's most meaningful moment." Many a Sunday morning came when I struggled to engage in the work of the day; it was always my Sunday morning routine of preparing my prayers that focused me for the worship at hand.

It is always a good test to ask whether you need to say something. If you don't need to, don't say it. This practice will serve you well.

17. Avoid a succession of loose sentences.

Strunk and White mean something very particular with this rule: a loose sentence is a two-clause sentence in which the two clauses are joined by a conjunction or relative (i.e., and, but, who, which, while, when, where). A succession of loose sentences can be rambling, even singsong. Sentences can be too short and periodic as well. A series of short sentences can become monotonous. Strunk and White stress that a variety of sentence structures works best.

For prayer, the goal is focus. Keeping the connections clear when we pray gives our prayers direction and clarity. This is especially true in public prayer, which can suffer from monotony and lack of direction. When praying in public, use precise, direct language to keep your listeners engaged in the prayer. Remember, the more focused you are, the more focused your listeners will be. Rhetoric is fine but don't overdo it. Plain speaking counts.

When I was a young boy, every Sunday one of the older men would pray during the worship service. Though I didn't realize it then, the pastor had asked one of them to pray and he had prepared for the moment. This prayer was meant to express the concerns of the congregation and balance the pastoral prayer. However, for a youngster, it was the most boring part of the service.

These older gentlemen (they were always men, at least in my memory) would pray with great elocution and bombast. I couldn't concentrate on what the prayers were about for all the words they used. They seemed to go on forever. Then, one Sunday a man got up and simply prayed for God to guide us and help those in need (some of whom he mentioned), thanked Him for the gifts of life, and sat down. I was stunned because I realized for the first time what those prayers were really about. Many times over the years, in many situations, I have prayed and thanked God for the gifts of life.

18. Coordinate your thoughts, feelings, and expressions.

This is simply a positive way of saying, "Don't ramble." The previous rules imply it, but it is always best to state such things plainly. More important, this rule keeps you on track. In worship, coordinating your thoughts, feelings, and expressions provides focus for formal prayers, such as confession or illumination, but there are times when the moment itself defines what is prayed. The event — a birth, surgery, or holiday — shapes the prayer. Other prayers cover more ground. They are more general. However, they too flow better and make more sense when they hang together, when they are coordinated. This goes for both public and private prayer.

So strive to keep language of the prayer in the same tone or at the same level: formal with formal, casual with casual. It is a different thing to pray in the midst of a high worship service or around a campfire. The feelings expressed should fit the subject of the prayer as well. Appropriate feelings are important in public prayer, and they should not jarringly shift from sad to happy. Not only is it disconcerting, it also raises doubt about the sincerity of the prayer.

A prayer, especially a personal or private prayer, may cover a wide range of topics. Coordinating the thoughts, feelings, and expressions keeps the prayer coherent, whether it is concise or general. That coherence helps the person praying stay focused and, should it be public, helps those listening to understand.

19. Do not summarize.

What you have prayed is prayed. You don't have to reiterate. God has heard it. If it's a public prayer, you're not responsible for the others getting it. That is their task. Do conclude, however. Address the Great Other to start the prayer; close with another acknowledgment. It gives the prayer a sense of balance and completion. A closing reminder that God is involved doesn't hurt either, but don't repeat the main points.

20. *Emphasize what is most important.*

Every prayer is different. Even when you pray a standard prayer such as the Lord's Prayer, it is not the same every time. The context makes a difference, be it a funeral, a wedding, Sunday worship, a family gathering, or your personal prayer time. Pay attention to what is important in that moment. What prompts the prayer makes a difference in what and how you pray. It shades, forms, and guides the prayer. The purpose of a prayer should be lifted up and made clear.

The prayers I share with my choirs before Sunday worship are example of purposeful prayers. This was something I didn't do early in my career. It started rather by accident — as God often works — in one church, yet it became an important part of my worship experience, and continued in the rest of my parishes. What this pre-worship prayer did was center the choir and myself on the worship ahead. It took into account the moment we were in, our reason for being there, and our common purpose. On the Sunday after 9/11 this prayer calmed us and gave us the sense of peace we needed to make the worship meaningful. Through this prayer, we recognized what was most important during that difficult time and what we had to do. It was prayer truly answered in the praying.

[3]

SOME MATTERS of FORM

One problem people have with prayer is its form. They believe or have been taught that there is a right and wrong way to pray. They think prayer must follow a particular pattern and contain all the right elements. On one hand prayer is seen to be formal — serious, straight-laced, following strict guidelines, used in the right way at the right time — and indeed there are appropriate times for formal prayer. On the other hand they see prayer as formulaic, following a particular pattern for a particular purpose, and, yes, some prayers have that design. So these worries about form are really not misplaced. Prayer carries a lot of baggage with it. People will often stumble over that baggage and then drop the whole effort out of frustration.

Two thousand years of tradition in the case of Christians and more in the case of Jews create ample opportunities for formal and formulaic problems to crop up. The key is understanding the nature and intent of both formal prayers and formulaic uses of prayer. When his disciples asked him how to pray, Jesus gave them what is known as the Lord's Prayer.

Did that mean that every prayer had to be the Lord's Prayer? No, of course it didn't. The Lord's Prayer covers the basics: honoring God, recognizing our physical and moral limits and obligations, and expressing our hopes. Now there's a formula for prayer. Is it scary? Is it difficult? Only if you have problems with those things, and if you do, then you better pray about them.

Many times over my years in the parish, people have said to me, "I wish I could pray like that." I've learned to tell them "God doesn't want you to pray like me; He wants you to pray like you." Being at ease with the formula and forms of prayer is one of a pastor's key skills; encouraging the prayer life is one of a pastor's essential tasks. In the church especially, formula equals ritual and the main purpose of ritual is creating pathways of communication with God. The trick for the regular person is to feel free within the ritual or forms so that what he or she expresses through them is significant and authentic.

This brings us to the dichotomy of discipline and freedom. Forms and formulas often appear to stifle individual expression and freedom. Ritual can prevent a person from expressing the full range of his or her concerns with God. However, ritual can also free a person to open himself or herself to God. Why? Because freedom and discipline are two sides of the same coin. Freedom without discipline is chaos; discipline without freedom is tyranny. Discipline is the exercise of freedom, while freedom is the exercise of discipline. Discipline is only effective when one can freely choose to act in a certain way. Freedom is only real when one determines and adheres to a certain set of actions. Again, freedom and discipline are inextricably linked to one another. So the forms of prayer should lead to the freedom of prayer and the freedom of prayer should be engendered by its forms.

Let's consider some of the forms and formulas that allow freedom and discipline to flow together in prayer.

Address. "Our Father who art in heaven," "Lord," "Oh God" — all these are examples of the address. The address simply sets the stage. It lets you and the One you address know what you are about. It reflects your frame of mind as you enter the process. Some forms of address work in certain situations but not in others. With personal prayers you should use the address with which you are most comfortable. Public prayer is more restrictive because you want use an address that includes everyone. Sometimes the form of the address can be striking and different, but it still needs clarity and purpose so people can be included. Think of Cool Hand Luke's final prayer when he calls God "Old Man." That's not a phrase that would work well in a public prayer, except maybe in a theatrical performance of a private prayer.

Amen. Amen literally means "so be it" and gives prayer a definite end, which it needs. Any prayer, public or private, must end and the person praying must be clear about that ending. The time for praying has concluded and the time now begins when the prayers, petitions, hopes, confessions, and decisions are to be enacted.

Grace. The grace before meals — not God's love, though they are intimately connected — is not a test or sign of faithfulness. Grace is meant to express thankfulness to God for sustenance both physical and spiritual. If you are comfortable saying grace in public, fine;

if you say grace in public to show off, not so fine. Grace is a good reminder of our dependence upon the Great Other's love; it is not false humility or a proselytizing tool. Use it when and where you feel it is most appropriate. If you are in a public situation, you might use more universal and less faith-specific language, such as, "For this bounty, we offer thanks."

Language. Use your language as much as possible. I mean the language you normally speak. Don't try to dress things up linguistically unless the occasion really calls for it. Unless you are naturally given to flights of rhetoric, don't try it. God would much rather have you be clear about what you are saying than have you be fancy. It's better for you too. If you are praying in public, it will go easier and better. If you are using a scripted prayer (see above) it's okay to translate it to fit your style of speaking.

Length. The situation determines the length of prayer. A lengthy prayer doesn't make you any holier. If you've got a lot of ground to cover then it obviously will be longer, but if you are praying about a particular situation, don't beat it to death. The most meaningful prayers are usually those that arise in the moment such as counseling the grief-stricken or celebrating a birth. They are short, usually less than a minute, and to the point.

Public versus private. In the best of possible worlds, public and private prayers would be the same, but we live in the real world. Public prayer brings with it certain needs that must be met to make it meaningful. It must be understandable, succinct, and engaging. It must also be appropriate for the situation and moment. Private prayer can be looser, more informal, because it is just you and God. Public prayer is you and God and any number of others. You cannot ignore that fact and still make the prayer truly significant. So public prayer must conform to more standard modes of expression. You can go into private prayer without preparation, but you should not go into public prayer without prior thought and anticipation.

Repetition. It is okay to repeat prayers. Remember, we repeat the Lord's Prayer, Hail Mary, or the rosary prayer all the time. Ron Del Bene devised the Breath Prayer, a prayer that takes one breath to pray, to aid people with particular situations or problems. They simply repeat the prayer when they feel the need. An example would be: "Lord, Give me peace." Over the years I've repeated prayers on liturgical occasions. If they fit, I use them.

Scripted prayers. The liturgical world is inundated with prayer books, resource books, and worship books containing written prayers. They may follow a theme or the liturgical calendar, which divides the year according to church seasons and festivals or the lectionary readings that cover the biblical story in a three-year cycle. They are great resources and there is nothing wrong with using them. They give good examples of prayers for all kinds of situations from worship services to bedside visits. If you are new to this praying business, check them out, use them. Don't be afraid to change them to fit your situation. Add to them; personalize them. The beans in the can don't do you any good until you open the can up and eat them.

Special needs. Prayers should fit the need and the moment. Very particular problems are often presented in prayer, and sensitivity to such needs is essential to making the prayer work for yourself and others. Listen to what is being said and raised and use that as the springboard for the prayer. Such petitions should simply be stated and given to the Great Other. An example: "O God, give (*name*) through your grace the strength to face this illness and the assurance of your love. In Jesus's name, Amen." Prayer should teach us to trust.

[4]

COMMONLY MISUSED WORDS, EXPRESSIONS, and CONCEPTS

A lot of theological and liturgical language is misunderstood, misused, scary, and deliberately obtuse. Such language can serve a purpose, but when it gets in the way of communicating about faith, that purpose gets lost. This chapter shows you how to keep theological terms from becoming obstacles to talking about faith. What follows is a little glossary of religious language often associated with prayer. It is not meant to be as exhaustive or definitive as a dictionary, that has been done better and more extensively in other places (see especially Frederick Buechner's books *Wishful*

Thinking and *Whistling in the Dark*). The intent is to inspire you to seek definitions that make the best sense for you.

Absolution. Despite what some might think, absolution is not wiping the slate clean of your wrongdoing. It is more like picking up another slate and starting a new chapter in a continuing work. What we seek in absolution is not forgetting the bad things we've done but ending their hold on us. It is a humbling moment because we have to realize that we are not capable of absolution on our own. The Higher Power, the Great Other, God does it, sometimes through intermediaries, sometimes directly. In absolution, our attention is turned from our past to our future.

Atonement. Atonement is the act of setting things right with the Great Other and yourself. If confession is the bridge that spans the gap created by sin between God and yourself, atonement is the act of walking across that bridge. It is taking the right relationship you establish with God into the world in which you live.

Belief. Belief is a commitment, more fundamentally the commitment that underlies our understanding of who and what we are (see Michael Polanyi's *The Tacit*

Dimension). All understanding is grounded in belief, even that of atheists. Without belief most of us wouldn't get out of bed in the morning.

Benediction. Literally the "good word," benediction is the send off to any worship experience because it is the final assurance that God is ultimately interested in our well being. It is the period on the worship sentence. It is the final reminder that we should have that same interest in our neighbors. No worship is complete without it, not even and maybe especially funerals. How appropriate that worship ends in prayer. For example: "May the Lord bless you and keep you, may the Lord shine his face upon you, may the Lord lift up his countenance on you and give you peace. Amen."

Catholic. Used to describe all denominations together, the word *catholic* defines the Christian universe. It intends to include not exclude. Like any good ideal it is more of a hope than a reality.

Confession. Confession is owning up, being responsible, or simply saying, "I'm the one who did this." A confession only makes sense if you are saying it to God, first and foremost, and that makes the phrase "prayer of confession" almost redundant. If you say it to God, you are the only other one who hears it, unless the transgression involves another person (as it usually does) and then you have to make amends (see *absolution* and *pardon*).

Creed. An odd kind of public prayer, a creed is directed not so much to God as to the community of believers, telling them how they are supposed to believe. The hope seems to be that God eavesdrops and approves of what He hears.

Discipline. Discipline is an act, freely chosen, that is repeated many times over. It requires commitment to behave in that particular, and sometimes peculiar, fashion. Its repetition never exhausts it possibilities because the exercise of discipline opens the possibility of new action. A prayer life chosen and enacted upon is a discipline and is essential in the life of faith.

Faith. Faith is a commitment that results in behavior and belief, which then shape your life and guide its direction. People have faith whether they know it or not. It is a verb disguised in noun's clothing. You don't adhere to it because you're supposed to, but rather because it gives or enhances life's meaning. Faith takes many shapes and forms, from deceptively simple to stunningly complex. At its heart, every faith, from atheism to Zoroastrianism, is an act of trusting that we are all involved in something greater than ourselves.

Freedom. The ability to choose between the options presented, freedom only becomes real when we reach decisions and make choices. Freedom always implies responsibility and requires discipline for its maintenance. Prayer that is freely offered is the only truly meaningful prayer.

Grace. Not to be confused with the pre-meal prayer, spiritual grace defines the underlying "givenness" of life. Grace is the primary act of freedom because God, the Great Other, the Higher Power, chooses to create and care for us, to give us life. God freely chooses that act of creation and it gives form to our lives. We are thereby given the same opportunity to create and care. Prayer is the fundamental conversation about producing grace in our lives.

Holy. The word for the presence of God, holy is something that happens, not something we control or evoke. It is sort of like being in the middle of something and realizing that you are between two mirrors creating an infinite progression. When you experience a holy moment you perceive the connection between what you are doing in that moment and the whole of creation. It can be scary, sad, ecstatic, even funny. Trying too hard usually prevents it.

Illumination. A prayer of illumination is usually used prior to the reading of scripture in hopes that we won't have to spend too much time trying to understand the scripture. This kind of prayer should be as constant in our prayer life as confession. Illumination is seeking to understand what God intends for us, whether we're reading scripture or talking to our children. The drive to illumination or understanding is part and parcel of what it means to be human. To seek it consciously is a wise thing, but be careful — answers and understanding are not always the same thing.

Incarnation. Incarnation is the Christian doctrine that describes the word becoming flesh, God becoming human, and makes the whole messy enterprise of life worthwhile.

Intercession. Literally, intercession means "coming between." It probably should be thought of as "caught in the middle." When praying for others the trick is not to think that your prayers are the means of their healing or salvation or whatever it is that you pray for. Your prayers of intercession are simply stating what you hope will be for those you have mentioned. Intercession is not faith healing; it is the reminder of what you would want to happen for yourself if you were in someone else's shoes. It is the first step in the journey of compassion.

Justice. The quality of a decision is judged by how well it considers all the factors and parties involved in the situation. Justice is restorative and brings balance to the situation. It is not vindictive. Prayers for justice can be general or particular; in fact, they should be both.

Mercy. Justice is something we do; mercy is something we give. Mercy is not possible without justice just as justice without mercy is ultimately pointless. If justice is the restoration of right balance in relationships, mercy is its fullest expression and sets a new beginning for them. Justice only takes things back to the way they were meant to be. Mercy goes further and says you can start all over again. We should pray that we can both give and receive mercy.

Pardon. Once you have confessed your sins, the next thing to do is ask for pardon from them. If we believe that God is both just and merciful, we should expect our sins to be pardoned, and during formal worship the liturgist will often demonstrate such trust by praying for the assurance of pardon. We should also expect such justice and mercy to become a part of our lives (see *absolution*). Pardon is not a get-out-of-jail-free card; it is a get-out-of-jail-changed card.

Prophecy. There have been towering theological debates about whether or not God knows the future. If He does, it is pretty clear He hasn't let us in on it. Prophets in the Old Testament were not fortune-tellers; they were truth-tellers. They were not interested in predictions as much as they were interested in consequences and faithfulness. Their orientation was less toward the future and what it might hold than on the now and what people, especially powerful people, needed to do to be faithful. It was a pretty harsh vocation when you look at the evidence. One must be careful when venturing into prophecy; you tend to end up in odd places (e.g., cisterns, caves, bellies of great fish, prison, a cross).

Religion, religious. I was once asked by an in-law whether I considered myself to be religious. I didn't know what to say and finally stuttered something about "no more than the next guy." Over time I discovered the truth of that statement and realized that religion is just a formal way of asking ourselves questions that clarify our faith.

When spelled with a capital "R," *religion* can get formal real fast. Unless we need to make the distinction between different religions, most of us are more comfortable with the small case "r."

Repentance. This is a name for the whole process of confession, pardon, and absolution. It is about the change of heart that leads from brokenness to wholeness at every level of life. If you start repenting in your prayers to God its healing effect will become active when you engage with others. The really cool thing is that it works backward as well. You can start by acting better toward others and end up telling the Great Other all about it. It is a dynamic relationship where each part can inform and shape the other.

Righteousness. This is more about getting it right than being right. The latter leads to self-righteousness, pride, and all kinds of other divisive attitudes. To be counted among the righteous, you must be trying to do the right thing and always wondering if you have. H. Richard Niebuhr called such an attitude an uneasy conscience and said the only proper stance before God was repentance. The truly righteous are sure about God and not so sure about themselves.

Sin. *Sin* is the name for the many ways we break the relationships of our lives. Original sin refers to the capacity we all have, and use, to do just that. No matter how you divide them up or rank them, our sins are one of the few constants of our lives. They are the central subject of our prayers whether we like to admit it or not, and the sooner we do admit it the sooner we can work things out.

Theology. Defined as the study of religious faith, *theology* literally means "God talk" or "speech about God." We tend to use the term in the latter sense, which causes problems because the speech is ours and we don't really know what we are talking about. The study of theology serves a purpose in helping us clarify what we are thinking and feeling, but it works best in the classroom or discussion group and should be avoided in prayers and most sermons. The hope is that the latter sense will give way to the former and that we will have the sense to shut up and listen.

[5]

An APPROACH to PRAYER

We now confront a mystery — indeed, the central mystery that arises in any good religion — namely, the relationship of the Divine with the individual. Prayer is how we comport ourselves in opening and contributing to that relationship. Up to this point our concerns have been with our use of and expression in prayer. Now we venture into a much less precise yet much more dynamic arena. We seek a personal approach to prayer. As Strunk and White say, we will be "steering by stars that are disturbingly in motion."

No single approach will work for everyone. The

expression that works for one will not work for another. The hope is that, no matter how the individual identifies the Divine, anyone who prays will find what works best for him or her, what fits, what makes communicating with his or her Higher Power comfortable.

That does not mean it is okay to allow idiosyncratic expression to become unintelligible. If you don't make sense to someone else you probably are not making sense to yourself or the Great Other, and while the Divine may know what you mean, it is just as important for you to know what you mean. That is what makes this mysterious conversation meaningful. In addition, you may, if you continue this habit of prayer, find yourself praying in public sometime. If you are comfortable praying in private you can be comfortable praying in public. They really are not all that different.

We now turn to a list of rules to guide our approach. They are intended to keep your journey on an even keel. They are not meant to be hard and fast. They are more reminders than strictures because each of us will approach prayer differently. That is a wonderful part of the Great Mystery of faith. Each one of those approaches can enlighten or uplift or sustain us. They can give us new perspective or new hope or new strength. To be able to connect to others in prayer is a powerful and empowering experience. It begins with connecting with God for each and all of us. It is my hope these rules will speed your journey.

1. *There is no star in prayer.*

Prayer is not about you making yourself the center of God's attention. Prayer is about communicating with the Great Other and communication is a two-way street. Information flows both ways. If your intention is to grab Divine attention, you are praying for the wrong reason. It is not about you taking center stage on some spiritual game show. It is about submitting yourself to seek God's will in your life. It is also not about making yourself the lead in a spiritual drama. It is about becoming the person the Higher Power means you to be. It is an exercise in humility.

Being humble does not mean being meek. In one of his sermons, author Clarence Jordan says that the Greek word used in the Beatitudes (Matthew 5) for "humble" is the same word used to describe being broken to bridle. He had known a number of mules broken to bridle, Jordan wrote, and none of them was meek. Submitting to the will of God does not mean giving yourself up; it means making your self stronger and most fully what you are meant to be. That takes courage, dedication, and hard work. Prayer is the central element in that process. That doesn't make you a star; that makes you human.

There is a strong, maybe even virulent, strain of narcissism in our society today. For many, the world revolves around me and the most important, most engaging matter is what I think and feel and believe. Our media plays to this narcissism with constant news stories that focus on individuals at the cost of explaining a broader context and create the need for individuals to be the center of attention. Prayer is the antidote to that attitude because it doesn't seek to aggrandize the individual. It seeks openness to God, which helps each person understand his or her place in the universe.

2. Listen to yourself first.

This does not contradict rule one. Listening to yourself first does not put you in the spotlight. Like rule one, listening to yourself first allows you to pray from a place of honesty and humility. In order to find your place you must start from where you are now. You must then ask the hard questions that submit your will to God's will. You are the only one who can ask them.

You don't want to sound false and you don't want to be false. That is not the way to humility before God. You want to be real and natural and honest. Only by listening to yourself first can you begin to move in that direction. The neat thing is that you can relax. Since you can't really fool the Divine you don't have to put on the masks you normally use to hide your true self. Simply be who you are and pray accordingly.

I had a friend in seminary who was fun to be around. We spent a lot of time talking and laughing late into the night. One night as we were watching the late news we got talking about what parts of our faith made personal sense to us. He confessed that he had a hard time with prayer and was simply not comfortable when he prayed. I got up and turned off the TV and told him to pray. He looked at me like I was nuts. However, I insisted, I couldn't comment on his praying unless I heard him do it. After some good-natured haggling, he acquiesced. He sounded stiff and formal and ill at ease. I asked if that was how he prayed privately. He thought for a few moments and said that was pretty much how he prayed all the time. I responded that he didn't sound like himself but more like what he thought would be a holy version of himself. He would be a lot more comfortable with prayer, I thought, if he just let himself be who he was.

Listen to what you pray and if it doesn't sound right or feel right, try again (see rule five below.) Prayer should be your most important communication and therefore it has to be honest and real. If you start there the rest of the journey will be a lot easier.

3. Use what fits.

This is not just about finding the right word. This is also about praying what is right for the moment and situation. As one of my teachers once said, "You don't say grace at a funeral." It is jarring to have someone pray in a fashion that does not fit the surroundings or the moment.

While that may seem obvious, this rule emphasizes the need to be sensitive. Being a pastor gives you free rein to pray at the drop of a hat. People expect you to, but it isn't automatic. You try to read what is happening, have some insight into why, and then proceed to pray accordingly. I once entered the hospital room of an elderly but active parishioner and found another visitor present. My parishioner introduced me to her sister and we all talked for a few minutes. During that conversation I picked up on a distinct air of tension between the two and realized this was the sister who was an atheist that my parishioner had mentioned in some earlier conversations. "In a family the size of mine," she had said, "there's always one who has to be different." I knew the parishioner wanted a prayer before I left, but I didn't want to increase the tension between the two. When it came time for me to leave, I asked the sister if she would mind if I said a prayer. She seemed startled, since her religious preferences had not been mentioned in the conversation. To her credit, she said it was fine with her. So I prayed for strength and courage in the face of illness and its uncertainty. I prayed that faith, in whatever form it took, would help us face this uncertainty. When I finished, my parishioner gave my hand an extra squeeze and me a knowing smile as I left.

Knowing what fits starts with knowing where you are and what is foremost in your heart and mind. If something is seriously bothering you, you don't stop worrying about it when you come to your prayer time. You include it.

You even feature it.

This self-knowledge helps when you are called upon to pray in public. You usually know where you fit in a group and what you can say in it. Public prayer extends that personal relationship, and one hopes deepens it. So you pray what fits the group. You would not offer the same prayer in your bible study group as you would in your social club meeting. It seems so obvious, but it is easy to forget.

I am not saying all prayer has to be planned. Obviously, when you are unexpectedly called upon to pray in public, you cannot plan too well, but if you are used to praying and use your common sense you can put the prayer into the appropriate frame. Likewise, there are times when you simply are not able to put yourself in the right frame to pray in public and it is okay if you don't.

4. Stick to the basics.

This is good general advice but it is especially important in praying. There is no need to get flighty or esoteric or arcane or anything else but basic when you pray. You can even say that prayer is the basic communication that makes all other forms meaningful. To use the language of theologian Paul Tillich, the Great Other is the ground of all Being, so by definition any communication you have with the Divine is basic. The only one you're fooling when you deviate from that principle is yourself.

This is just as true with public as with private prayer. Sticking to basics meets our need for the central elements of the spiritual life: forgiveness of ourselves and others, the strength to carry on, the search for God's will in our lives, gratitude for the gifts of life, and praise for the Great Other. Sticking to these elements always works. In addition, you won't fool anyone if you get too full of yourself. Groups are almost as good as God at picking up on insincerity. Besides, sticking to basics makes for shorter public prayers, which counts for a lot.

5. *Revise your prayer until it feels right.*

My wife is a novelist and knows full well the importance of revising. It is the real work of writing. Everybody may do it differently, but we all revise our thoughts and prayers in some fashion. It is very rare for someone to sit down and have a creation spring whole and full-blown from his or her mind. Poet John Keats did not simply sit down one day and record "Ode to a Grecian Urn." It took labor and revision (and probably some revision after that).

You may ask, but aren't you supposed to pray from the heart? Yes. And the mind. And the soul. There have been times when I've had to pray when my heart just wanted to scream or cry or laugh. Prayer is about finding the words to express what most involves the heart and soul and mind. There have been times when I have screamed and cried and laughed before God, but I came back to those emotions and restated them as prayer, sometimes repeatedly, until I knew I had gotten them stated right. The very act of revising a prayer is prayer and can lead to new insights and greater understanding.

Praying in public is not necessarily any different.

When you are expected to pray in a group, prepare for it. Write or plan the prayer, put it aside, come back to it, and go over it. Do that as many times as you can stand until it sounds good to you.

During my years in the parish, I would often use books of liturgical prayers to prepare for Sunday worship. They usually gave me written prayers attuned to the day's scripture, but I almost always revised those prayers, be they invocations, pastoral prayers, or prayers of confession. I would work to make them fit my congregation and sometimes even individuals. It was always gratifying to have a parishioner tell me that he or she had found a prayer meaningful after Sunday worship. If Christians are supposed to always have uneasy consciences, as theologian H. Richard Niebuhr proposed, then pray-ers should as well where preparation of their prayers is concerned.

6. Use simple words.

You are not trying to impress anybody when you pray. You are trying to communicate with God. If you're concerned about showing off your vocabulary, find a different place to do it. Just as with writing, simple words are usually just as expressive as complicated ones.

I love words. I enjoy their interplay and their shadings of meanings, but I learned early in my career that fancy, complicated words have limited use in communication, especially spoken communication. While I might have a significant conversation with a colleague about ontology and soteriology — why I would, I don't know — most people would not readily understand these theological terms. My high school chemistry teacher once handed me a card that read "Eschew obfuscation. Venerate perspicacity," which proves its own point. Over the years I learned that when I use a "big" word, even if it is the best word for the job, I should explain or define it. In prayer I keep the language simple.

Why? Because I don't want to distract people from the main purpose of praying: communication with the Divine. I don't want them stumbling over the language when the focus needs to be on the Higher Power and their relation with it. The same is true in personal prayer, just more directly. I don't want to be stumbling over my language and worrying about how I say something when I should be focusing on my meaning. Sometimes the right word can be a big word. The more you keep things simple the more likely you'll be able to recognize which words add meaning to your prayer.

7. Keep your expression measured.

When you pray you do not have to score rhetorical points. There is no scoreboard for grandiose statements.

This is true whenever and wherever you pray. When you overstate something you detract from its importance. The facts will speak for themselves, the emotions aroused will seek their own level, and the meaning will come into focus. You cannot by dent of overblown language add anything to that, in public or private. When you pray, keep yourself and your language on a level plain; the way you seek will be more discernible.

Some people when they pray, especially in public, make a great show of emotion and flowery language. While they may feel that it is genuine (and indeed, it may be genuine for them), it too often strikes me as what Rex Stout's fictional detective Nero Wolfe would characterize as "flummery." Try to remember the contents of one such prayer. Then think of Abraham Lincoln's Gettysburg address, or his second inaugural speech, or John Kennedy's inaugural address. We remember them mainly because of their measured and simple expression.

8. Don't hedge your bets.

It is hard, maybe impossible, to overemphasize the safety of prayer. Safety is not even a good enough word. Sanctity says it best, and the old meaning of the word, rooted in the idea of a place where no harm can come, is truly the heart of the matter. Prayer is a time of sanctuary. That is why most of us worship in a church. Sanctuary doesn't mean that a place is holy; it means it is safe. Holiness may make it safe, the invoked presence of God may ensure safety in that place, but first and foremost a sanctuary is where those who gather are free to be themselves and without fear of harm.

Prayer is such a gathering wherever it occurs. It is a gathering of you and the Great Other. When you gather with God, you are safe. You can be who you really truly are, because you are with the One who intends that you be. So you can be totally, completely, utterly honest and say whatever you want. God will not punish you for the conversation. God wants to hear what most troubles you, what most injures or angers or frustrates you, what most encourages you or heals you or empowers you.

One of the holiest moments I've had was a simple walk on the coast of Maine with a long-time friend whom I had not seen in a while. It was sunrise and we navigated the rocky coast along the bay in front of our cottage. As we reached our destination, the point that protected that stretch of coast, the sun rose and set the sky and sea on fire with light. We stopped, almost stunned by the beauty of it. He turned to me and said, "I feel like praying," which was unusual for him. So we did. And we both were as honest and open as we could be. We were safe and trusting in the face of such beauty.

With that kind of safety you don't need to hedge your bets. You don't need to explain your statements. You don't need to justify your ideas or feelings. They are what they are and prayer is about presenting them to your Higher Power.

9. Don't be flippant.

I often have to remind myself of this one. For whatever reason I have a strong tendency to make wise cracks, and it has caused a number of problems over the years. I once made an offhand remark in a Bible class while discussing how different sides of a person's character can be depicted. Our discussion reminded me of a phrase, an old album title I think, that went "you are never alone with a schizophrenic," and I used it in our discussion. It was only after class was over that I remembered that the only son of one of the couples present had recently been diagnosed with schizophrenia and was trying to rebuild his life. Despite apologizing to them in private, I still cringe when I think of that one.

While people are less likely to be flippant in a private prayer, it is much easier in public prayer. The temptation may arise from overconfidence or a lack of confidence or some other insecurity. Flippancy is a short cut, and doesn't work in public or private prayer because it disrupts the focus and flow of the prayer. It focuses attention on the one praying, not the prayer. It is self-centered, prideful, and violates rules one (there is no star in prayer) and four (stick to the basics). It is condescending because it forces the listeners to think about what the one praying knows rather than what he or she is praying about.

The point is that prayer is a communication between you and God; it is not about you making yourself the center of attention or trying to alleviate your insecurities.

10. Ground your prayer in orthodoxy.

Orthodoxy from its roots means "right speech." Right speech is what praying is all about. Finding the right words and meanings to express is the work of prayer. Think of Jesus in the Garden of Gethsemane: he prays "remove this cup from me, yet not what I will, but what thou wilt."(Matt. 26: 36–46) This expresses his feelings and his understanding accurately and compellingly. When we pray we are attempting that "right speech" with the Divine.

This is not a theological rule. The great anthropologist Clifford Geertz said when writing about theory that "short flights of ratiocination are best." He meant that one should never venture too far from the data or facts or observations in the field. The same could be said for theology and prayer. You do not need a lot of theology to make a meaningful prayer and you are better off leaving it out all together. Prayer is not a place to make theological points. We have sermons and papers and books for that. That doesn't mean that prayer is not a hotbed of religious change. It means that prayer is more fundamental than theology.

Theological and religious change may spring from prayer as issues and ideas are presented and considered there, but that process should not be wild-eyed and chaotic. It should be humble and measured. It should be thoughtful and respectful. This is not to deny the deep emotional elements involved in such issues. We have to recognize those, but we must strive to present them to God in the right way. The prayer life of Martin Luther as he prepared and presented his Ninety-five Theses must have been full of deep emotion, but it probably was not chaotic and wildly expressive.

It is okay to fly off the handle in prayer. There are certainly biblical examples; Jeremiah, who was always complaining to Yahweh, and Jonah, who defies God, come to mind. The struggle then becomes how to tame that expression into an idea or concept that is more understandable and thus more amenable to the way we seek with God. We have to question why we prayed in that way, what provoked that outburst, what is at stake that moved us to that depth of feeling? We find a place for it, and the best way to do that is standing on the firm ground that keeping our prayer life orthodox provides. It provides the baseline to which our freedom is attached when it is necessary to express great emotion. We may venture off that baseline but we should always try to return to it. Such grounding keeps our journey in faith on a steady course.

11. Show what you mean.

This might be better stated as "present the facts." When you are praying there is no need to dress things up and overexplain them. Like the writing maxim "show, don't tell," remember that you don't need to tell about what you need, just say it. "Little Jimmy is sick with a cold. Help him through this hard time, Lord, and give me the grace I need to help him," is much better than "Little Jimmy has caught cold, Lord, and can't go to school and is not used to being laid up and so he is all fidgety and whiny and driving me crazy. I need all the help I can get." Showing what you mean helps keep you from wandering off the path. If you are praying in public it keeps everyone else on the path as well.

12. Keep it smooth.

This rule flows naturally from the preceding rule, "show what you mean." If you spend a lot of time, energy, and thought on telling all about what you are presenting in prayer, you will create long, meandering prayers. By focusing on showing the issues, ideas, and events your prayer will flow more smoothly and you'll avoid sidetracks and stumbles.

Keeping it smooth means finding a way to communicate that feels comfortable and easy for you and allows you to say what needs to be said so that all involved are clear on the subject.

This is not the same thing as being slick. We have all had the experience of meeting someone who can sell ice to Eskimos. There are people who can talk and talk or write and write and not say anything worth remembering. When the speaker is self-centered or self-aggrandizing, his or her communication will tend to cause confusion and put the listener at a disadvantage.

Being slick is about being manipulative; being smooth is about communicating well. Manipulation has no place in prayer because its purpose is to take advantage and cause hurt. Remember, prayer is a sanctuary, a safe place. Trying to manipulate God in private prayer harms the manipulator; trying to manipulate other people in public prayer violates the sanctity of prayer.

13. Be honest and self-contained when you pray.

This rule seems self-evident. Honesty is the cornerstone of prayer because it engenders responsibility. If you are honest with the Divine, you are honest with yourself and vice versa. Such honesty establishes the lines of responsible action. When you lie to yourself and therefore the Great Other, you only disrupt the sanctuary of prayer and prevent it from working.

This rule especially applies to prayers of intercession. When you bring up the plight (or the joy for that matter) of others in prayer you need to remember that it is your prayer and not theirs. If you over-identify with the beneficiaries of your prayer, you will fall into codependency. Real concern for others eventually reaches a point where you must let them find their own way through their problems. You can help, maybe in very significant ways or maybe by getting out of the way. However, you cannot solve someone else's problem. Your prayer should be about how to find the best way for you and them to enable healing or growth.

14. Use poetry carefully.

We sometimes confuse poetry for prayer. They are analogous. Poetry is to language as prayer is to life. Poetry goads language to change, opens new possibilities for expression, and upholds the strength of language. Prayer induces us to change our lives, opens new pathways, and supports the right way for us to go. They both require dedication, commitment, and hard work to get them right.

Prayer and poetry are not equivalent however. They have different ends and so to use poetry in prayer can be a tricky endeavor. Using a poem just because it sounds or feels good is not enough. It must fit the meaning of the prayer, its intention, and its goals. In public prayer, poetry must also reflect the language and expectations of the congregation. It is very easy to lose people when phrasing gets complex.

Using poetry in prayer requires is a good ear. You develop that by reading a lot of poetry and trying it out for yourself. There is plenty of poetry out there that is religiously oriented and even a fair amount written as or for prayers. You'll find there are times when poetry works and times when it doesn't. It may work just fine for you personally, but not in a public setting. To determine when to use poetry in your prayers, ask yourself, "does this poem add to the prayer or distract from it?"

15. Express yourself clearly.

This does not mean that you will always have a clear and definite idea when you pray. There are times when confusion rules and that is what you present to your Higher Power. There will be moments when emotions roil and tumble your psyche and soul. When they do, bring these emotions to your conversation with God. Strive to be clear with them. Do your best to state these confusing emotions clearly. You will benefit from the effort; you will gain a measure of understanding that will help you cope with those tumults. If you stumble, start over. If you are overwhelmed, let the emotions roil and tumble for a while, then try again to present them clearly.

I was called to the bedside of a dying man and many family members were gathered round. It was just a matter of time before he died. The couple had been one of my favorites in that parish, always a delight to visit. It was hard to stand there with the sobbing family and the unconscious man and wait for death to come. I was there to pray and to pastor, but as I stood there with my arm around the wife's thin shoulders all I could feel was grief and sorrow. We all talked in desultory fashion for a while, some stories were shared, a few brief smiles. I felt the wife's hand grip my shoulder and I knew it was time to pray. I asked that we all pray silently for a time, allowing me to marshal my feelings and thoughts. Then, I prayed aloud, stating as simply and as clearly as I could what I was feeling and what I needed from God. Her grip tightened as I prayed. When I finished we all stood silently together for a few more minutes. His breath finally slowed and stopped and the attendant nurse pronounced him dead. The family said their good-byes.

The feelings I had were tumultuous, but praying silently for a time gave me the opportunity to put them in order, to identify what was happening to me emotionally and gain a sense of composure so I could share my feelings and thoughts with the family. I was able to present them and make them available to others. It was this sharing that got us through that time. In *The Wounded Healer*, author Henri Nouwen says that the function of ministry is to deepen pain so that it might be shared. Praying clearly is an essential act of such ministry.

Ambiguity is dangerous. It can lead to misunderstandings and miscalculations. It can cause wrong decisions and misperceptions. It can lead to disruption and even death. There is a huge difference between a sign that says "Rough road ahead" and one that says "Bridge out." Tragedy lurks in ambiguity. Be clear and make sure you have said what needs to be said.

16. Avoid opinions.

We all know what an opinion is; everybody has one. Someone defined an opinion as a conclusion drawn despite the evidence. Opinions don't do you much good when you pray because they are more usually concerned with your ego than your soul. Prayer is not a place where you promote or support your opinion. It is a place where they will probably get straightened out.

17. Keep figures of speech at a minimum.

In the play of language and thought figures of speech, metaphors (e.g., argument is war), and similes (e.g., eyes like stars) play an interesting role. They can illuminate or obfuscate, they can create or hinder change in the language itself. They are the character actors of language, fulfilling a role but never taking center stage. That is why they are called supporting actors.

When you pray, figures of speech can get in the way and they should not be used if you are simply trying to make the prayer sound better in public. It is easy to get lost in a maze of simile that deters praying. Things get mixed up and people can easily lose their sense of what is happening if they are thinking more about how something was said rather than what was said. Praying is not about showing how well you can compare one thing to another.

Figures of speech can help depict a feeling or a thought. If a figure of speech helps you understand and be clear, then that is fine. If you use them in public prayer, question their usefulness. You can even try them out on someone beforehand to see if they work. Figures of speech usually take a little bit of mental digestion, and when you use them you have to allow for that. They can develop their own momentum and you can easily overdo it. That way leads to madness or even worse, mixed metaphors (i.e., teaching your mind's eye to play by ear, living high on the cob). The best policy is moderation.

18. Avoid shortcuts.

Praying should never be a burden or a task in which you search for labor-saving methods. Prayer is its own reward, and the time you spend praying is always time well spent. You don't need to worry about prayer getting in the way of some other part of your life. If you do, then you are praying for the wrong reasons. When you feel the need to leave something out of your prayer, the best thing to do is ask yourself why and pray about that. Odds are you are shying away from something you need to face and deal with. The time spent in prayer is God's time, or eternity. It is the time when you are in the presence of the Great Other. God's time resembles a climate more than a clock and should be experienced, not measured.

When you pray, include all the issues or needs you are aware of. Don't try to weigh one against another and think that the lesser ones can wait for another time. Give them all due consideration, pray for all of them. You have nothing to fear, remember? Prayer is a sanctuary. Everything, even the smallest concern, has a place there. Pay heed to that.

Learning how to include all your concerns in prayer takes discipline. It takes time. Think of that time as an offering to God. Make a commitment to pray each day for a certain amount of time. Keep that commitment, even if there are empty moments where you have nothing to present. Let that time fill up with God even in silence. In Genesis, Yahweh gives the world its full due in creation; He takes the whole six days and doesn't try to get it done in four. If He had, it would have been more about His power than His love. Prayer has that same quality, it is about how you love not how easily or quickly you do it.

Public prayer has different constraints, but the rule still applies as far as the group's needs are concerned. Whatever the situation, from study group to Sunday worship, the time involved is still God's time and the whole of the group's needs must be given an opportunity for expression. Allow for that when you pray publicly.

19. Use normal language.

Think of the Lord's Prayer, the Sarum Prayer, or the prayer of St. Francis Assisi. They are all simple prayers using straightforward language. Once they are in your mind and heart they stay there because these prayers express our reality in such vivid and telling ways. They are models of prayer that we can follow with our own language and our own reality. Their immediacy, cogency, and vitality are the hallmarks that all our prayers should emulate. That is made possible through language that does not venture into uncharted waters rife with hazards and hidden traps.

I used to say that some of the standard prayers in my denomination's prior book of worship reminded me more of insurance policies than prayers. I preferred the newer, more current prayers. However, over the years I came to see that those prayers had a stateliness and gravity that worked for certain situations and conditions. As I reread them I realized they didn't sound as much like insurance policies as I had thought, the language was not esoteric, just stately. The fault lay with my perception not the prayers. It is best to stay the steady course of normal language when praying, and keep an eye toward the horizon.

Approaching prayer is finally a matter of the person and not the method used. Everyone must find their own way if they are to find a way at all. Praying is an act of faith and no amount of trickery or snake oil will ease the way. It must be done with commitment, discipline, and hope or not at all. My way cannot be your way. These rules are not intended as a method or a formula to a successful prayer life. They are not exhaustive of all the things you encounter in a life of prayer. My hope, indeed my prayer, is that they will be helpful as you undertake that journey. May they keep you steering toward the end we all seek.

A SHORT CONCLUDING
UNSCIENTIFIC POSTSCRIPT

I f you have read this far it is because you are some-how called to prayer. A need stirs in you to reach out beyond yourself in order to understand yourself. This call can take many forms. Great tragedy, great joy, a sermon, a walk in the woods, the touch of a lover, the support of a friend, an experience that opens new vistas in your reality — the list is as infinite as we are. Whatever elicited your interest in prayer tells you, or maybe just hints to you, that you are involved in something greater than yourself. Prayer is the attempt to enhance that connection.

Notice that I use the phrase "called to prayer." All religions in some form call their followers to engage in prayer. They formalize or ritualize this essential part of the religious life. For many that form of public prayer is enough to establish and maintain the spiritual connection their faith describes. For many others that connection elicits a more private response and personal prayer takes a central role in the operation of their faith. These people develop their own rituals and routines for praying.

I grew up in a family that said grace before every meal at home. This family ritual instilled in me an attitude of thankfulness for what I had received and I am sure played no small part in my subsequent quest to understand the life of faith. Even there, I was called to prayer in the simple act of being called to eat. Countless times in my parish career, someone has said to me, "I feel I should pray about this." The word *should* is the indicator of being called. An obligation is being invoked or a need is being expressed. One's attention turns from just myself to myself and something else — something greater, something bigger, something that I need in order to understand who I am.

So we receive the summons, or possibly we feel lured forward, outward. But we are inevitably drawn toward a reality that not only includes us but also is greater than we could have imagined. We may not know this as we start out, but we soon discover it. Frodo and Sam are not sure where their journey will take them when they set out on the road that leads from Bag End, but they encounter more than they ever thought possible. Lucy and Edmund are not sure what they have stumbled upon when the go behind the wardrobe, but they set off on a journey into a vast and mysterious and wondrous world. Huckleberry sets off on the great river not knowing where it will lead, but confronts a reality more complicated than he thought possible.

The list goes on; you can pick your own heroes. The point is that we too set off on such journeys when we are summoned to prayer. We too are called upon to act, to suffer, to grow, to sacrifice, and finally to learn more about who we are and what we can do. In the end, that is what all good journeys do. They help us become who we most truly are and what we are truly meant to be.

Who then issues the summons? Who calls us to prayer? I have taken pains not to characterize the Deity in any consistent way — the Great Other, the Higher Power, the One, God. There are many other ways to name Deity. While you may take this as an indication of tolerance on my part, it is also the admission that I don't know who calls you forth to prayer. The God who calls me will not necessarily be the One who speaks to you. It may be the same One, but our perspectives will be different. The manifestation of the Great Other will not be the same for both of us. That is part of the Great Mystery and one of the things that makes the journey so exciting. You are always discovering more about the One who summons you. The more you discern of the One, the more you are likely to discern about yourself. That seems to be the way it works. You must find the way that works for you, the way you can most comfortably pursue your journey.

The image of a journey or quest or pilgrimage works best for this undertaking since it underscores its continuing nature. We don't experience our journey's end on this side of the grave. We never have all the answers or all the solutions. We keep seeking them. Like I said, I don't know who calls you forth. I can't even prove that the One is out there calling you. That's why I call this little conclusion unscientific. It is not about proving anything. It is not about marshalling evidence and data to uphold a position. It comes from an older tradition, one that depends on witness and witnessing, on telling the story as you know it, as it has been passed on to you and changed by you from your experience.

Prayer is central to that journey. It may be that the prayers of formal worship are enough for you to steer by, or you may need to engage more actively in your navigation. Or you may find yourself somewhere between these two. Whatever the case, prayer is an essential part of that endeavor in life we call faith. It will not give you proof. It may not provide a lot of answers. Having prayer answered and finding answers are two different things. However, it will see you through; it will give you a light to steer by and a course to follow.

What I have offered here is more of a sample guideline than a list of commandments that demands strict obedience. Part of the journey, a very important part, is figuring out your own guidelines. I believe this is one of the reasons that throughout his ministry Jesus consistently implores his listeners to have ears to hear and reminds them that they themselves must decide what to do. Prayer will launch you onto the uncharted sea of your life and part of your task will be devising the means of charting it.

It is my hope that this little book will help you in that effort, as a model for your own approach. Prayer is not to be feared; if this book has helped you overcome any hesitancy about prayer, then it has achieved its purpose. Further, it is my hope that prayer will, if it hasn't already, become a vital part of your life. It is my hope that you will embark on this journey of faith and find that while answers may not be abundant, life is.

That as you seek the way, it will, as the Quakers say, open before you. That as you pray compassionately, you will find yourself being compassionate. That you will strive to be faithful through your prayers, and that through your prayers faith will find you. It is my prayer that along your journey you discover such hope for all. If this little book helps you in this way, it will be an answered prayer.

ACKNOWLEDGMENTS

There are so many to whom I owe thanks for the production of this book that I cannot name them all, friends, parishioners, and colleagues. I would especially like to thank my mentors in the faith: Richard Whitworth, C. Glenn Mingledorff, David Giles, and Robert H. Spain. I would also like to thank my mentors in understanding the faith: Paul Deats, Leroy Rouner, and Harrell Beck. I must use prayer to thank Richard, Glenn, David, and Harrell, for their spirits walk in broader worlds.

I am particularly grateful to my agent, Denise Marcil, for her faith in this project and to her competent and gracious staff for all their help. Deep thanks go to my editor, Jason Gardner, for his sure hand, keen eye, and patience in leading a neophyte through the process.

My love and thanks go to my children, my daughter, Kate, and her husband, Conor, and my son, Zachary, for keeping me on an even keel. Most of all, my thanks and love go to my wife, Carla, for keeping faith in me through it all.

NOTES

xi   ...*teaching people to pray is teaching them to treat*...
Eugene H. Peterson, *Subversive Spirituality* (Grand
Rapids, MI: Eerdmans, 1997).

4   ...*the source of reality rather than morality*...Parker J.
Palmer, *Let Your Life Speak* (San Francisco: Jossey-Bass
Publishers, 2000).

24   ...*eternity is not the opposite of time but its essence*...
Frederick Buechner, *Wishful Thinking* (New York,
Harper & Row, 1973), 23.

27   ...*seeking and recognizing the presence of God*...Eugene H.
Peterson, *Subversive Spirituality* (Grand Rapids, MI:
Eerdmans, 1997).

36   ...*foresee and determine the shape*...William Strunk and
E. B. White, *The Elements of Style* 4th ed. (New York:
Longman Press, 2000), 15.

38   ...*Brevity is a by-product*...William Strunk and E. B.
White, *The Elements of Style* 4th ed. (New York:
Longman Press, 2000), 19.

40   ...*Doubt is the ants in the pants of faith*...Frederick
Buechner, *Wishful Thinking: A Theological ABC* (San
Francisco: HarperSanFrancisco, 1970).

55   ...*a prayer that takes one breath to pray*...Ron Del Bene,
The Breath Prayer (Nashville, TN: Upper Room Press,
1996).

67   ...*steering by stars*...William Strunk and E. B. White,
The Elements of Style 4th ed. (New York: Longman
Press, 2000), 66.

69   ...*mules broken to bridle*...Clarence Jordan, *The Substance
of Faith and Other Cottonpatch Sermons* (New York:
Association Press, 1972).

81   ...*short flights of ratiocination*...Clifford Geertz, *The
Interpretation of Cultures* (New York: Basic Books, 1973), 24.

88   ...*the function of ministry is to deepen pain*...Henri
Nouwen, *The Wounded Healer* (San Francisco:
HarperSanFrancisco, 1969).

RECOMMENDED READING

What follows is a personal reading list, a list of books that have personally affected me in my prayer life. It is not intended to be exhaustive or exclusive. It is idiosyncratic in the sense that it exhibits my personal spectrum of influences. Hopefully, it will help you determine your own list.

There is a vast number of books on the market concerning prayer. My own denominational marketer has forty-three Web pages of books under the heading "Prayer." You should feel free to range widely in seeking works that speak to your personal needs and interests regarding prayer.

Different kinds of books are included in this list: books of prayers; books about prayer and "prayerful books"; and books that engender prayerful thoughts and thoughts about prayer. I intentionally left out books on any specific theology or philosophy, with one exception: I have included Walter Brueggemann's books, which are based on his Old Testament theology, since they reflect an informative and inspiring path toward integrating our textual heritage and our faith.

My hope is that this list will help propel you in your quest for a life of prayer.

Baillie, John. *A Diary of Private Prayer*. New York: Charles Scribner and Sons, 1949.

Barclay, William. *Prayers for the Christian Year*. London: SCM Press, Ltd., 1964.

Bernanos, Georges. *The Diary of a Country Priest*. Translated by Pamela Morris. New York: MacMillan, 1937. Reprint, New York: Carroll and Graf, 1983.

Bloesch, Donald. *The Struggle of Prayer*. New York: Harper & Row, 1980.

Bonhoeffer, Dietrich. *Life Together: The Classic Exploration of Faith in Community*. Translated by John Doberstein. New York: Harper & Row, 1954.

Brueggemann, Walter. All titles, most published by Fortress Press, Minneapolis, MN.

Buechner, Frederick. All titles (which range from autobiography to fiction to sermons to essays), most published by Harper & Row, New York.

Campbell, Joseph. *Thou Art That: Transforming Religious Metaphor*. Novato, CA: New World Library, 2001.

Carretto, Carlo. *The God Who Comes*. London: Darton, Longman and Todd, 1981.

———. *Letters from the Desert*. Maryknoll, NY: Orbis Books, 1972.

Chariton, Igumen, of Valamo, comp. *The Art of Prayer: An Orthodox Anthology*. London: Faber and Faber, Ltd., 1966; reprint, 1997.

Crossan, John Dominic. *Raid on the Articulate*. New York: Harper & Row, 1976.

Fosdick, Harry Emerson. *The Meaning of Prayer*. Nashville: Abingdon Press, 1982.

Heschel, Abraham Joshua. *God In Search of Man: A Philosophy of Judaism*. New York: Farrar, Straus and Giroux, 1955.

Holmes, Urban, T. *Ministry and Imagination*. New York: Seabury Press, 1976.

Hopkins, Gerard Manly. *Poems and Prose of Gerard Manly Hopkins*. Selected by W. H. Gardner. New York: Penguin Books, 1953.

Job, Reuben, and Norman Shawchuck. *Guide to Prayer*. Nashville, TN: Upper Room Press, 1983.

Kazantzakis, Nikos. *The Saviors of God: Spiritual Exercises*. New York: Simon & Schuster, 1960. (See also his works of fiction.)

Lewis, C. S. *Mere Christianity*. New York: MacMillan, 1952. Reprint, New York: HarperCollins, 2001.

———. *The Weight of Glory*. New York: MacMillan, 1949. Reprint, New York: HarperCollins, 2001.

MacDonald, George. *Diary of an Old Soul*. Minneapolis, MN: Augsburg Publishing House, 1975; reprint: 1994.

———. *Life Essential: The Hope of the Gospel*. Wheaton, IL: Harold Shaw Publishing, 1974. Reprint, Vancouver, BC: Regent College Publishing, 2004.

Marshall, Peter. *The Prayers of Peter Marshall*. Edited by Catherine Marshall. Lincoln, VA: Chosen Books, 1954.

Norris, Kathleen. *Dakota: A Spiritual Geography*. New York: Houghton Mifflin, 1993.

Nouwen, Henri J. M. *A Cry for Mercy: Prayers from the Genesee*. New York: Doubleday and Co., 1981.

———. *Reaching Out: The Three Movements of the Spiritual Life*. New York: Doubleday and Co., 1972.

———. *The Wounded Healer*. New York: Doubleday and Co., 1972.

Palmer, Parker J. *Let Your Life Speak: Listening for the Voice of Vocation*. San Francisco: Jossey-Bass, 2000.

Pascal, Blaisé. *Penseés*. Translated by Honor Lévi. Oxford: Oxford University Press, 1995.

Peterson, Eugene H. *Subversive Spirituality*. Grand Rapids, MI: William B. Eerdmans, 1997.

Quoist, Michel. *Prayers*. Franklin, WI: Sheed and Ward, 1963.

Rilke, Rainer Maria. *The Book of Hours*. Translated by Annemarie Kidder. Evanston, IL: Northwestern University Press, 2001.

Warren, Robert Penn. *New and Selected Poems, 1923–1985*. New York: Random House, 1985.

Yeats, William Butler. *The Collected Poems*. New York: MacMillan, 1956.

ABOUT the AUTHOR

Joe B. Jewell, a Methodist pastor for over twenty-five years, has served in churches in small towns and large cities. He attended Vanderbilt University and the Boston University School of Theology. He lives with his family in Vermont.